A MAN'S WALK WITH GOD

S0-AZI-614

*A Study of the Process
for Faith's Progress and
Practical Development*

by JACK HAYFORD

Published by Living Way Ministries
14300 Sherman Way
Van Nuys, CA (USA) 91405-2499
(818) 779-8180 • (800) 776-8180

ISBN 0-916847-12-8
Printed in the United States of America

*This message was originally brought
at The Church On The Way.*

*It has since been edited and revised
for publication by Pastor Hayford,
in partnership with Pastor Bob Anderson,
Director of Pastoral Relations.*

*The audio cassette of this message
(#00486)
may be purchased from:*

*Living Way Ministries
14300 Sherman Way
Van Nuys, CA 91405*

TABLE OF CONTENTS

CHAPTER ONE:

THE POWER OF ALTARS–
HEART-TO-HEART
ENCOUNTERS WITH GOD

I could take you to the very spot where it happened.

I doubt that it would strike you as a particularly holy place. In fact, by appearance alone most anyone would call it "common" or "mundane."

I'm talking about a special point on Interstate 405, north-bound, near the Victory Boulevard offramp. That's where it took place.

That's where I'll always remember it.

That's where God met me in a unique way.

That's where He spoke words to my heart--highly significant words regarding my future; words which turned out to impact both my own and the future of God's purpose for a church congregation. It's the same one I've now served for nearly 25 years since that moment, so the importance of the encounter is obvious.

That section of freeway will always remind me of that divine encounter.

For me, that stretch of pavement is an altar.

Not Just the Wooden Railing

If we look at godly men of old and observe their encounters with the Most High God, and observe those places where God intersected their lives; in pivoting the course of their destinies into a new direction, one thing stands out.

Altars.

At the point of their encounter, it's there that you'll find an altar--a clear milestone erected in one form or another.

Say "altar" and most people picture furniture. But I'm not talking about furniture in an ancient tabernacle, an area in a cathedral, or a wooden prayer rail in front of a church platform. I'm actually not even yet speaking about a physical stone pile, as with the case of our text which relates to Abraham's altars. Please understand--all the above *are* legitimate expressions of an altar, but at the mere human plane. None of these sites or symbols alone by themselves has the intrinsic power to:

• Alter the direction of a human life,

• Change the fabric of a person's character,

• Shape the realization of someone's destiny.

I have no problem with wooden railings or high altars in churches, nor qualms about other devoted sanctuaries of human consecration. Altars, as a means to worship and prayer, are sometimes imperative and often revitalizing. However, I *do* have a problem, as I'm sure you do, with religious artifacts--places or practices--that lose their original power and significance because mechanical routines have replaced spiritual vitality with human traditions.

Many of us have past experiences in church where kneeling at an altar was something you always "just do." I've been in churches where a Sunday service couldn't conclude without the leader proclaiming, "Now everybody, let's all come down to the altar in front." Sometimes it was dynamic, but other times it was merely a habit; a weekly re-verification of something no one seemed quite sure of. And often, after about two minutes, most of those who "came forward" were already up and gone. In five minutes, the whole place was empty.

Such habits usually hark back to a time when the power of God *did* visit people; when contrite, seeking souls came and were on their knees before the Living God at those altars for *hours*. But "glory eras" pass, or new seasons come, and each one calls for its own refreshing, lest we merely exercise routine habits devoid of wholeheartedness, diligence, or understanding.

Altars.

To some, the word may only sound religious. Uninteresting. Conjuring images of candles, incense, and genuflection. Yet altars have time and again been the very threshold for the power of God to pour forth on earth to people who have met God at one. They've met the *Living* God, in *living* faith, and entered a *living* relationship, and realized *living* experiences. These *altar experiences* frame the context in which Heaven's power invades hellish dominions; the setting in which God's Spirit penetrates earth's heartaches. Altars have set the conditions and met the moment in ways which have resulted in Christ's Lordship being expanded through human vessels. They have become thresholds of glory; glory which has poured forth into believers' lives as they are shaped under God's hand . . . at an altar.

Altars *are* thresholds--the footings of a doorway--because Heaven's power does not pour forth from a giant garden hose in the clouds. It opens its grace and pours forth over this planet through people like you and me who will find a place to meet God, and then *kneel* there and *knock.* Altar experiences with the Lord create within us new capacities; we become *wider* apertures, *larger* channels of grace, more *generous* and *powerful* conduits of the Holy Spirit. At the doorway of Heaven we find the doors of our being swung open to God, private quarters unveiled, heart secrets revealed, and God's life-power released to us. None of us can experience that without altars.

God's Word shows Abraham as a *prototype*--a first-of-a-kind person, who models through his own learning process what it means to walk by faith. Abraham's fruitfulness in life clearly came forth through a succession of "altars"--through dynamic encounters with God. He learned a walk with God that can teach every one of us today as well; but we will find one inescapable fundamental: *The unalterable need of an altar.*

At the core of a man's walk with God is each man's readiness to meet God *personally:*

• To answer the summons on your soul when He deals with you, rather than to subvert or rationalize His dealings and attempt an escape from His direct points of correction, instruction, or conviction.

• To be ready to submit to the Holy Spirit, whose relentless operations in our life are always to bring more and more of the likeness of Christ into our living through His faithful disallowance of things we would excuse, and His regular call to principles our flesh seeks to escape.

This pathway of walking with God has a distinct individuality to it. No one can walk this way as your proxy or substitute. In a way, it might be said that it's the ultimate *true* path of rugged individualism, in the most spiritual of terms. It's the place a man "gets to know God for himself," and where God truly "gets the man for Himself."

But before we probe further along this very biblical pathway of "spiritual rugged individualism," let me establish an imperative point of balance.

Anyone familiar with my ministry knows that I put great emphasis on the practice of people getting together and praying with and for one another. It's scriptural. It's powerful. Its benefits have been proven unerringly. However, truth out of balance becomes error.

So in keeping wise checks and balances in place on this issue of a man's walk with God, let me be clear. I would not want for one second to deter anyone from the valid and proper place of regularly going to another brother or group of fellow Christians and saying, "Will you pray with me?" Nor does the path we're probing avoid the honesty and humility in acknowledging to peers, "I'm facing something tough; could we get together and talk about it?" I wouldn't want to seem to dissuade anyone from seeking godly counsel within the Body of Christ to obtain help in a difficult time.

In fact, I *encourage* that practice. However, I find that today this is an increasing substitute for personal encounters with God, and bearing each other's burden was never meant to lead to a dependency. I think that we need to perceive the difference and learn the place of both--prayer's fellowship, partnering with others; and prayer's partnership, fellowshiping with God alone.

Actually, it is plain wisdom to seek the strength of brothers and sisters. You'll likely die spiritually without it. But when that becomes a habit or substitute for a growing private walk with God, something within your spiritual life either never develops or will begin to atrophy. If I don't learn to draw on His well-spring of life within myself, I'll not learn the resource that will enable me to be His hand of strength to others. If I find I've become only a consumer and not a supplier by God's grace in me, it's probably due to the fact that I haven't been meeting the Lord often enough at my own altar.

Further, many of today's Christians need to learn most of their problems simply aren't going to be solved in a counseling office or in an effort at a quick-fix session of interaction with another believer. As valuable as such practices and spiritual human resources are, *most* of my life-problems and need for life-answers will only be solved on my knees before Jesus Himself! Coming into the presence of the Lord and finding an encounter with Him, from which point you go away *never the same again* with regard to that particular problem in your life, is an indispensable practice. His presence is the place where our hearts are *"altared"*--i.e., *put on the altar,* and as a result our whole lives will be *altered.* [Note the spelling difference: we're al*tar*ed to be al*ter*ed!]

These pages are not aimed at learning a ritual piling up of stones, kneeling at wooden railings, or sticking markers on the landscape. But there is a quest to build altars. And the goal is to facilitate a walk according to God's Word, pressing all of us into a liberating and life-changing understanding of altars as meeting places with God. Because we are dealing with issues of the heart and its intimate responses to God, an altar can range anywhere from a fireplace hearth, to a spot on the beach or in a field, to a profound encounter when you were alone with the Lord at a booth in a donut shop. God is everywhere and some of His most *altering* dealings with us happen in surprising settings, and sometimes when we weren't expecting it at all. That message is seen clearly in the life of Abraham.

As with you, dear brother, the Word of the Lord came to this man to reveal to him his divinely-appointed destiny. That Abraham learned to believe God, and to continue to hear God speak, is because Abraham learned to continue to build altars--to respond to God and to submit to His deal-ings with his soul. The very fulfillment of a man's *destiny* is contingent on his own *heart* being progressively changed, steadily being expanded to receive and embrace God's unfolding purpose in his life.

So it was with each altar Abraham built to the Lord. As his heart was altered--shaped and grown--his full destiny was being received from the hand of an eternal God and brought into reality in this tempo-ral world. It's a prototypical case of a man learning to walk with God.

TALK ABOUT IT! Chapter questions to discuss with a friend.

1) Even though you might not have realized they were "altar experiences" at the time, share an example of when you *knew* the Lord divinely directed your course in life and *how* you knew it was the Lord (ex-amples: where to go to college or what to study; whom to marry; what profession to enter or a career change; priorities with your family; etc.).

2) Discuss why it is so important that we continue to build altars throughout our lives.

CHAPTER TWO:

THE PURPOSE OF ALTARS--
MILESTONES OF
GOD'S DEALINGS

Every altar has its own application, its own story, its own purpose in God. And most dramatically, every altar has its own potential of a power-encounter to change one's life. That's the reason I'd like to ask you to walk with me through an examination of eight "altars" in Abraham's life. A few of them do not recite the word "altar" but they are all, nonetheless, very significant and strategic intersections of God's dealing in his life. Each of them speak pointedly to the process and the unique values of "altars" in a man's life, and to the way they build and advance his walk with God. While we'll study these eight altars over the course of the following chapters, let's first get a panoramic view of the altars Abraham built to God.

The essential elements of the life of Abraham, "the father of the faithful" can be read in a matter of minutes. In most Bibles, the whole of his biography occupies little more than a dozen pages. Let me encourage you to read it all at once--perhaps this evening. In about 30 minutes you'll have reviewed the primary details of a very ordinary, sometimes fearful, always faithful man--who learned to walk with God. Beginning at Genesis 11:27, read through Chapter 22. *

As you read, note these eight "altar" occasions:

Altar 1: Genesis 12:7** - This occurs when Abraham first comes into the land of the Canaanites, after God issues His call to him.

Altar 2: Genesis 12:8 - Though immediately approximate to the preceding altar in the text, there would have been a time-lapse between the two occasions.

Altar 3: Genesis 13:4 - Abraham returns from the confusing trip to Egypt, and now reestablishes the altar he earlier built.

Altar 4: Genesis 13:18 - Again, no measured passage of time is given, but sufficient time had elapsed to occasion the growth of his flocks (vs. 6). God is now giving a more explicit perspective on the earlier promise of "the land."

---

* Other details continue through Genesis 25, but they are not primary to Abraham's lifelong pursuit of God's will.

** Though he is first called Abram, we will consistently refer to Abraham by the fuller name God eventually gave him (see Genesis 17:5).

Altar 5: Genesis 14:18-24 - No altar is specified, but in his saying, "I have lifted my hand to the Lord," describing his worship at Melchizedek's direction, Abraham references an encounter with God that has long-term implications.

Altar 6: Genesis 15:1-21 - Verses 9-10 specifically describe the sacrifices offered, so although the word "altar" doesn't appear, it is clear that one was employed. Again, we are probably looking at a time passage of at least months, if not years, between these "altar" encounters.

Altar 7: Genesis 17:1-27 - In the establishing of the covenant of circumcision, Abraham's encounter does not report a stone or earthen altar being built, but his own body becomes marked by the will to worship and sacrifice to God.

Altar 8: Genesis 22:1-19 - This event, probably 35-40 years into Abraham's advancing walk with God, occasions the highest "altar" of his lifetime because of the powerful prophetic picture it gives of Christ, and because of the glorious seal it provides to Abraham's faith-walk.

With this summary in mind, we're about to look at the power-principles for a growing walk with God as demonstrated in Abraham's life. But before we do, let me make three encompassing statements. For as surely as Abraham's life teaches us POINTS of power, there is something of vast importance to be learned about the PRO-CESS of God's power in a man's life. Please note:

• THE PRINCIPLE OF TIME: Abraham's encounters with God as they appear in the altar experiences noted in the Scriptures covered a period of at least 40 years. This is not suggesting that "every five years" God met him on an appointment basis, since eight incidents are in focus. But it should help us to see that a maturing walk with God involves God-given time for growth.

• THE PROBLEM OF FEAR: Abraham's arrangement with Sarah, that she lie about their relationship whenever they were in a hostile setting that might threaten Abraham's life, is certainly unbecoming. Yet the patience of God with a fearful man should be noted. In short, the Bible makes clear that God's ability to build a man of faith is *not* removed because at earlier points in his walk with Him the man has struggles with fear.

• THE PRIORITY OF RESPONSIVE-NESS: Abraham's faith is the product of his readiness to respond to God. Though he is called the "father of faith," he did not arrive at that title by reason of a grand exercise of mighty spirituality. All he does is simply answer when God calls. Even though he is sometimes apparently fearful and even though his development takes decades within his lifetime, the essence of his faith is in the fact that he *responds* to God, rather than hides from His call.

Let these three factors weld themselves into your soul, dear friend.

You are clearly interested in becoming a man with a growing, effective walk with God. That interest is a strong beginning. But the above insights will prove, I've learned, *very* essential to maintaining patience and perspective. So, with that foundational counsel in place, let us begin looking at the individual altar-encounters of Abraham--as we learn from these milestones of God's dealings with a man.

A Man's Altar of Promise

How does God whisper *promise* to a man's life?

There are many ways, but the most common is a direct utterance from His Word--The Bible. You're reading one day, and a phrase, a text, an incident in the Scriptures JUMPS OUT AT YOU! Suddenly, it's in strobe lights: your heart leaps, or is warmed, and you KNOW--it's not simply "biblical," but it has suddenly become *personal*.

It may have been in a service as the Word of God was being taught. Or the text of His Word may have become electrically alive as the Holy Spirit breathed a "word" of prophecy, and the exhortation underscored a *truth; your* truth from *His* Truth--The

Word alive, for *you.*

This is God's way; something He delights to do--to make His Word a promise of purpose, power, and destiny to *you.* As surely as He first wants to make His Son ours as personal Savior, He wants to build our walk with Him at a personal level as He applies His word--*personally!*

God isn't in the generalizing business. He gets specific, and His Word is filled with promises He wants to press into a place in our hearts so that we will each know for certain: His promises not only are *true,* they're for *me!*

Abraham's experience was exactly like this, with but one exception. At the time he lived there was no written Word of God. Still, the Lord spoke to him, and in Genesis 12:1-7, we're given the beginning of His doing so: the setting, the promise, and Abraham's response.

Now the Lord had said to Abram: "Get out of your country, from your family and from your father's house, to a land that I will show you. I will make you a great nation; I will bless you and make your name great; and you shall be a blessing. I will bless those who bless you, and I will curse him who curses you; and in you all the families of the earth shall be blessed." So Abram departed as the Lord had spoken to him, and Lot went with him. And Abram was seventy-five years old when he departed from Haran. Then

Abram took Sarai his wife and Lot his brother's son, and all their possessions that they had gathered, and the people whom they had acquired in Haran, and they departed to go to the land of Canaan. So they came to the land of Canaan. Abram passed through the land to the place of Shechem, as far as the terebinth tree of Moreh. And the Canaanites were then in the land. Then the Lord appeared to Abram and said, "To your descendants I will give this land." And there he built an altar to the Lord, who had appeared to him. Genesis 12:1-7

It's essential in learning a man's walk with God that we grasp two important things from the onset. First, there is *promise* seeded in the call God gives in inviting you and me to that walk. Second, there is *purpose* for each of our lives which is waiting to unfold.

Listen to God's words to Abraham, and inherent within them I'm asking you to hear His voice to you as well. From the text of Scripture quoted above, take a pen and fill in the phrase from His words to Abraham, and apply them to yourself.

• God's promise is to BLESS you (12:2a).

_____

• God's promise is to do something GREAT with you (12:2b,c).

_____

• God's promise is to MULTIPLY you (12:3).

• God's promise is to give you a PLACE in His purpose (12:7).

I can't urge you strongly enough to lay hold of this first principle: GOD WANTS TO BRING YOU TO A PLACE OF PROMISE, AND SEAL THAT PROMISE AT AN ALTAR OF ENCOUNTER WITH HIM! In other words, He wants you to be so confident that He *means* to bless, multiply, and bring you to largeness of purpose in His will, that you will let this become a covenanted matter with Him.

That's what constitutes the milestones of a man's walk with God. It is staked out by the altars--the places, times, and moments when you *hear* God speak to your heart about His purpose for you, and you *agree:* you *receive* and *seal* that covenant in an altar-like encounter. Let me illustrate.

Earlier, I mentioned a moment in time on the 405 Freeway in the San Fernando Valley area of Los Angeles, and an "altar" encounter I had with God there.

It was a crystal clear afternoon, two weeks after that Wednesday in March over two decades ago, when my wife and I had accepted a short, interim pastorate of a small church in Van Nuys. As I drove northward, having left the print shop where I'd placed a small order for church bulletins (we only had about 20 people in the congregation), I had little on my mind other than a comfortable drive back to my office.

Suddenly, without any premeditated thought on my own mind, other than that my eyes had scanned the "bowl" formed by the surrounding mountains hemming this portion of Los Angeles, the Holy Spirit whispered: " This is your valley." The impression was clear and the meaning was obvious, though I could fathom no way to apply it. "Your valley" meant "The place of your assignment, and the intended location of God for your ministry."

As I said above, *I thought* I was on an interim, temporary deputation assignment to oversee a small congregation for a six-month span of time. Little did I know God had charted the course of my destiny for this place, and for many years to come.

My response?

It was very, very limited--as limited as my understanding at that moment. And because of my limited point of view, all I did was take the words to heart--accept them for whatever God meant them to be, because I certainly didn't understand them myself.

As it has turned out, God has done remarkable and mighty things in making that small congregation into a global ministry center which serves the entire San Fernando Valley as well. But that day, all I knew to do was *receive,* to let my heart (which had other plans than this valley) keep open to God's purpose.

And I tell this simple story because it's a practical testimony.

1. It illustrates one man's "walk" in opening to a forward step with God, even though he doesn't know where the path will lead. (That's what Abraham did--Hebrews 11:8.)

2. It illustrates the way that God's promise doesn't need to be understood in its fullness in order to be received at its beginning. [Abraham at first was told he would become "a nation" (12:2), then "like the stars" (15:5), and even later "a father of many nations" (17:4).]

3. It illustrates the fact that a simple "present yourself at the altar of openness" is all that's needed. From that point, the heart has released God to bring about His higher purposes in the man to whom He has spoken.

When God said to Abraham, " To your descendants I will give this land," the next words we read are: *"And there he built an altar."* To build an altar is to agree with God:

• Accepting His promise for your future, and committing to walk forward with Him toward its fulfillment.

• Laying your life in openness before

Him as the Lord of your life's issues and as the Master of your destiny.

Listen, dear brother in Christ! This is crucial to a man's beginning a faith-walk with God. Let me share it with you just as I spoke it at one of our men's gatherings.

   *   *   *   *   *

Now, men, notice God says, "To your descendants I will give this land (vs. 7). . . Go to a land that I will show you" (vs. 1).

Do you see that?

God gave him a *promise*. He promised him greatness, significance; that He was going to do something with his life to bring him to an appointed destiny.

Does that sound familiar? It should because that's exactly what the Lord says to you and me. He says, "I call you to come out and follow Me. I'm going to make you amount to something. I'm going to bless you. I'm going to bless people through you. And I'm going to bring you to an appointed place--a destiny that I have fashioned for you."

That's God's promise to you and me throughout Scripture, since God's Word speaks of us as the spiritual offspring of Abraham. In Romans 4:11-13 we're referred to as the spiritual progeny of Abraham, and he's a kind of prototype of all of us . . . the people of faith.

26

Now, in our text (12:7) Abraham arrives at the *place* of his destiny and God says, "Abraham, this is the place! I'm going to do something with you here; *even though it hasn't happened yet, this is the place!*" God makes His promise firm. It's tagged to a specific point. And when Abraham might later feel the temptation to doubt, he can look at that stone altar baking in the noon-day sun or towering in the moonlight; stones which could whisper, "Remember the day I was built? God spoke to you. And what He promised *will* happen!"

Brother, what has God said to you? Let's apply it.

Build a Milestone of Remembrance

Rather than stones, take up pen and paper. Abraham didn't have the convenience of a computer or a stationery store down the street, but we do. And I would urge every disciple of Jesus Christ to benefit from keeping a spiritual journal. Men who walk with God have always done this: Martin Luther, John Wesley, Hudson Taylor, Jonathan Edwards--the list goes on and on. Such men kept notes on God's dealing with them.

Words from the Lord to your own heart, as edifying as they may be, can easily lose their power and sustaining grace in your life if they are not set in place--written down. It's like placing the stones of an altar. Such pragmatics can be intensely spiritual and powerful in daily life.

Listen, when God speaks to you, you can be sure the Adversary of your soul will be quick to sow seeds of doubt each time the Lord gives you His word. "Has God said?" is a famous line from hell--one which even Jesus had thrown at Him by the devil. But when the record of God's personal dealings with you is in ink, it's much easier for you to point to the journal, and reply to hell's host or your own doubts:

- "Yeah? Look right here--page 15!"

Or,

- "I was standing right under the oak tree at my uncle's house reading the Bible!"

Or,

- "It was March 19--That's when that scripture came alive--right out of the Word for *me* that day. I *knew* it and I *know* it!"

Hell has to back off in the face of that kind of confidence at such "altar" moments. So, establish that wisdom, brother. As a man committed to a walk with God, secure the wisdom of keeping a spiritual diary, recording things the Lord has shown to you or promised you. These texts show it to be both practical and scriptural:

Then the Lord answered me and said: "Write the vision and make it plain on tablets, that he may run who reads it. For the vision is yet for an appointed time; but at the end it will speak, and it will not lie. Though it tarries, wait for it; because it will surely come, it will not tarry."   *Habakkuk 2:2-3*

I will remember the works of the Lord; surely I will remember Your wonders of old.   *Psalm 77:11*

Remember His marvelous works which He has done, His wonders, and the judgments of His mouth . . .
    Psalm 105:5

A Man's Altar of Prayer

The second altar Abraham erected secured another principle in his life. It was a principal key as he learned a man's walk with God.

And he moved from there to the mountain east of Bethel, and he pitched his tent with Bethel on the west and Ai on the east; there he built an altar to the Lord and called on the name of the Lord.
    Genesis 12:8

Abraham *called on the name of the Lord.* That's the *first* time we have direct reference to Abraham's calling on the Lord by His *personal* name. The significance of this is that his prayer enters a new dimension of

29

intimacy in his knowledge of the Lord.

The language of that time contained names for the Lord that focused on His role as Creator-God and as The Almighty One. But here is the personal Redeemer-God-- Yahweh--the One who will become mankind's Savior. In a real and powerful sense, Abraham is getting to know God in a new, deeper way; perceiving more of His character and Person.

Coming to know more of God's way as you walk with Him is born of coming to know more of God Himself! Psalm 25:14 says, "The secret of the Lord is with those who fear Him, and He will show them His covenant." This, too, is a call to altar-building; but it isn't a one-time encounter. It's a progressive discovery of coming to more of a "first name" relationship with the God who has called you, who has promised to work His purpose and power in your life.

Further, will you notice, Abraham "moved . . . " (12:8). Make no mistake, Sir. A man's walk with God doesn't stagnate. The issue isn't geographical movement, but *forward* movement--advancing in the knowledge of God's Son, His ways, His heart, and His Spirit. Hear the Apostle Paul say, after having walked with Lord for nearly 20 years, *"That I may know Him!!"* Listen to those words, because they echo the sound of the man who has found the *way* of beginning with God, but who wants to move unto the *wealth* of knowing Him--MORE!

How is this altar erected? Probably the simplest specifications are in the answer, "morning by morning."

Try an experiment. This is not a law, nor a legal requirement for true spirituality. It's an experiment. And the goal of the experiment is to prove in your own experience the faithfulness of James 4:8 which says, "Draw near to God and He will draw near to you." Here it is:

Set your alarm clock 30 minutes earlier than usual--60 if you dare. Begin to spend a newly devoted block of time weekday mornings--worshiping, meeting, talking with the Lord . . . just "drawing close" to Him. I say that risking the danger that someone will interpret this as a legalistic demand for true spirituality, or as if providing a magic span of time will achieve familiarity with the Almighty. But my guess is that the Lord has already been dealing with your heart about spending even *more* time before Him. If He's telling you to expand to 15 minutes, honor that. If it's weekly, daily, or three times a week, just do what He says. In any case, cut new ground.

Pursue the Lord. Set your new regimen for a three-month target. Then, at the end of that time, see if that altar of prayer hasn't shaken loose something of the "old life" and, in exchange, fostered a fresh invasion of holy intimacy you've never known with the Lord before!

I issue this bold challenge, trusting that you will understand my point: the issue is a dynamic pursuit of the Lord, not a legal edict mandating a time-span. I want to urge you, brother: ask the Lord how *He* would have *you* pursue Him at the altar of prayer. Then build it--and expect Him to meet you there.

A Man's Altar of Permanence

We're told exactly why Abraham went south to Egypt: "There was a famine in the land" (12:10); but there is one highly important *missing* piece of information. Nowhere does it say, " The Lord *said,* 'Go to Egypt.' "

There is a common feature to most of our personal biographies: *we wander without wisdom.* It doesn't happen all the time. It doesn't happen because of an indifference toward walking with God. But it does happen, and it is usually because we come to circumstances where our *survival* seems at risk and our *seeking* is sacrificed. Let me share a testimony of a "near miss" I had along this line.

My wife, Anna, became pregnant with our first child just seven months after we entered the ministry. It wasn't a very opportune time, seeing as our salary was very slim and our tiny congregation hardly established at all. As the early months of her pregnancy went by, we hoped we might be able to save for the costs of the baby's birth, because there was no insurance resource available at that time. Then, with only six weeks left until the due date, I became restless.

"Honey," I said, "I'm going to get a part-time job on the side. I know it will remove time from my studies and pastoral responsibilities, but we need the money."

I was also concerned that I not be a bad example by appearing to the other families in our small flock to be slothful. I reasoned, "If I don't do something to see these costs covered, some of the men--especially new believers--will think 'faith is irresponsible.'" And I remember how it was in this mood that I took the morning newspaper in hand that wintry morning, to look for a job.

Equally clear is the memory of the inner pressure as I began to search the paper for job opportunities. It was a clear tug on my heart which made me extremely uncomfortable. No words were spoken to me, but a heaviness came upon my soul that only lifted when I prayed, "Lord, I think I understand what You're doing. You're *stopping* me from launching out on a path of my own wisdom, and You're calling me to trust You with this matter."

Though it's been years since that day, it's a well-defined moment when I was called to build an altar of *permanence*--to establish the fact by faith that I was called to do one thing in the will of God, and that probing other pathways was not His plan--no matter *how* "good" the motive or purpose seemed. I have no idea what distraction or confusion I may have avoided, but I do know the marvel of the miracles of God's provisions that eventuated, for when our first child arrived--a sweet little girl!--we had enough to (1) pay off the doctor and hospital completely, (2) buy basic supplies for setting up a home with "new baby equipment," and (3) provide 6 weeks of the special canned formula prescribed by the doctor for feeding our child. It was thrilling!! And it was an early lesson in "walking with God" and avoiding "wandering into Egypt."

Abraham's trip to Egypt wasn't without a logical reason, but when we study the whole text, we find his venture leads to manipulation and compromise. Read the story.

Now there was a famine in the land, and Abram went down to Egypt to dwell there, for the famine was severe in the land. And it came to pass, when he was close to entering Egypt, that he said to Sarai his wife, "Indeed I know that you are a woman of beautiful countenance. Therefore it will happen, when the Egyp-

tians see you, that they will say, 'This is his wife'; and they will kill me, but they will let you live. Please say you are my sister, that it may be well with me for your sake, and that I may live because of you." So it was, when Abram came into Egypt, that the Egyptians saw the woman, that she was very beautiful. The princes of Pharaoh also saw her and commended her to Pharaoh. And the woman was taken to Pharaoh's house. He treated Abram well for her sake. He had sheep, oxen, male donkeys, male and female servants, female donkeys, and camels. But the Lord plagued Pharaoh and his house with great plagues because of Sarai, Abram's wife. And Pharaoh called Abram and said, "What is this you have done to me? Why did you not tell me that she was your wife? Why did you say, 'She is my sister'? I might have taken her as my wife. Now therefore, here is your wife; take her and go your way." So Pharaoh commanded his men concerning him; and they sent him away, with his wife and all that he had.

Then Abram went up from Egypt, he and his wife and all that he had, and Lot with him, to the South. Abram was very rich in livestock, in silver, and in gold. And he went on his journey from the South as far as Bethel, to the place where his tent had been at the beginning, between Bethel

*and Ai, to the place of the altar which he
had made there at first. And there Abram
called on the name of the Lord.*
Genesis 12:10 -13:4

There are two lessons this "return-to-
the-altar" experience of Abraham teaches
us: (1) *Don't* wander via human wisdom,
but *do* walk in God's (12:10-20)! (2) *If*
you've wandered in presumption, igno-
rance, or confusion, you *can* return to the
altar of God for reestablishment (13:1-4)!

Learning to walk with God calls us to
learn to heed the inner signals of His
dealing, to expect progressive calls to new
levels of sensible, biblical faith. The altar of
permanence doesn't need to be built *after* a
trip to Egypt. You can build your altar of
permanence *before* drifting into confusion
and compromise through not trying to solve
your problems by journeying according to
your own map.

"But," someone says, "it appears that
Abraham returned *richer* as a result of his
Egyptian junket, even though he stumbled
into compromise!" And the truth of the
matter is that it *does* seem he did. But we'll
miss the grander points of the text if we
presume that God's prospering was a sign
of pleasure, when in fact it was a signal of
His incredible mercy.

There seems to be a principle of God's
dealings with all of us who choose to walk

with Him. If we *will* to walk in self-willed paths, we insure unfruitfulness. But if we *stumble* onto dead-end streets in the learning process, God doesn't approve of the detour, but He will mercifully bring us out--and we'll profit from the lesson. And, by the way, as to Abraham's increased wealth from his time in Egypt (12:16, 20; 13:2), please remember that God didn't need Egypt's help to provide for Abraham's well-being!! Just as I learned long ago through the incident of being "stopped before Egypt" as the baby's arrival drew near: God-Our-Provider is capable to meet needs and abound *without* the assistance of human wisdom's enterprise!

Listen, dear brother. There is someone reading this page right now who has fumbled and slipped into Abraham-like patterns of compromise and confusion. You wonder how a man like you who wanted a walk with God got in a place like this; also wondering if there is a way you can return to a compromise-free, unencumbered-by-Egypt walk.

The answer is YES! And the place where you've met God at the altar *before* simply waits for you to come and rebuild the altar *now*. Never let the Adversary of your soul tell you otherwise!

Dave had returned from Viet Nam, and when I saw his face in the service that night I could read his thoughts like a book. His guilty face seemed to say: "I've been gone so long. Failed so foolishly while overseas:

compromised my commitment. I'd love to return to the fullness of the Lord's way, but I don't deserve to do so." It was as though he felt he needed to earn his way back to God.

When my message was concluded, most everyone in the room had knelt at their seat to enter into the regular prayer-meeting format for this midweek night. But I went down from the platform to where Dave was seated, head buried in his hands. I simply whispered, as I leaned over to his side:

"Dave, it's not a mile or a thousand steps to come back, it's only *one*--one step from where you are to where Jesus is--right now."

He looked up, his eyes flashed with hope, and he stood and took one step--into my arms, and then both of us went to the altar to pray.

Today, Dave is a gifted Christian counsellor, his home a center of vital joy and life in Christ, for that night he *came back*--and built an altar of permanence.

It can be built *before*, by hearing God's wisdom.

It can be built *after*, even though you've wandered.

And the earnest, humble heart wanting to walk with God will be profited by His abundance of grace and mercy!

**TALK ABOUT IT! Chapter
questions to discuss with a friend.**

1) What *realistic* goal do you
feel the Lord leading you to make for
spending time with Him in prayer
over the next three months? Be
specific: decide when, where, how
long, how often, etc.; and write down
your commitment below. Remember, this may be different for each
person--there is no *right* answer;
the key is to commit to *expanding*
your present prayer pattern.

2) Discuss the benefits of keeping a spiritual journal. Commit to
devote part of the prayer time above
in writing down your thoughts,
prayer requests and answers, Holy
Spirit-given insights, and even questions about situations or circumstances you don't yet understand.

CHAPTER THREE:

THE PRACTICALITY OF ALTARS—FACE-TO-FACE WITH DEITY

I could reel off the names of half a dozen teachers I've had and another half dozen authors, who have dramatically touched my life at significant times. I could also talk about many individuals whose personal lives, counsel, teaching, example, or ministry has been a great blessing to me; people whose words greatly helped, at moments when God used them to speak a phrase or reach with a touch that proved to be a point of great personal release and encouragement. Without question, there is a place for *people* teaching and strengthening one another.

But I want to also tell you that the major points in my life--the moments to which I return and say, "*That* is the point at which there came a turning; *that* is the time when my life moved into a whole new realm; *that's* the occasion when solid things were anchored in my soul" . . . *those* are usually times when I have been *alone with the Lord.*

He is the Central Personality for us all-- the One ready to progressively shape life under His touch when He can find a person--a *man*--who will walk with Him from altar to altar. There aren't short cuts. There are simply some things that the Lord is just jealous enough to not let anyone else get in on. He wants to have the hand in the establishing and firming up of some things in our lives that will happen no other way.

• We won't get it by running to another meeting;

• It won't come by listening to another tape;

• You won't get it by going to another counselor;

• I'm not going to find it by any device, regardless of how positive or beneficial that resource may be.

But you and I will find that our "next step with God" at such times is by one means--*alone*: Coming to the Living God and building an altar!

A Man's Altar of Possession

Let's read Abraham's fourth altar experience:

The Lord said to Abram, after Lot had separated from him: Lift your eyes now and look from the place where you are; northward, southward, eastward, and westward; for all the land which you see I give to you and your descendants forever. And I will make your descendants as the dust of the earth; so that if a man could number the dust of the earth, then

your descendants also could be num-
bered. Arise, walk in the land through
its length and its width, for I give it to
you. Then Abram moved his tent, and
went and dwelt by the terebinth trees of
Mamre, which are in Hebron, and built
an altar there to the Lord.
Genesis 13:14-18

Abraham--a man learning to walk with God--is a man whose life is increasingly being marked by a trail of altars. Similar to a string of lights etching the outline of an airport runway at night, his altar fires served as a holy means by which God escorted him into the destiny to which He had called him.

Each altar testifies as a monument to something the Lord is speaking or doing in his life. At key moments altars are built and become witnesses that God has spoken. In this fourth case, the altar becomes direc- tion in his life to move him another step toward possessing his destiny. This altar, in a very real sense, becomes a weapon of warfare.

The striking thing about this altar en- counter in Abraham's evolving walk with God is that the altar so very inescapably links God's *promise* of the land (13:14) with a call to *prophetic action:* "Arise, walk in the land through its length and its width, for I give it to you" (13:17).

"Prophetic action" is action taken in the physical, visible realm because of something we believe about the spiritual, invisible realm. Abraham was told a promise of future possession--*now* he *acts* as the possessor, and he builds an altar to commemorate the act.

Such action moves beyond the *idea* of God's promise to the actual conviction that His promise is in action--*NOW!* It's wise to see the practical, nonsuperstitious nature of such action. Both passivity and unbelief scoff at such actions as Abraham's: "Walk through the land?! What difference does it make? If God's going to give it to him, He's going to do it anyway!" But God isn't wasting words or playing games. He's moving Abraham from ethereal, intangible notions, to solid, faith-securing convictions.

There's a good deal of innocuous, indecisive religious habit today. Maybe a degree of sincerity rests at the roots of such spiritual passiveness, but too many believers don't know or don't think it important to anchor promises to a firm foundation of action; to *possessing* the promise by faith's participative act. And seldom do they learn to tack down their experiences in meeting God by building altars. Consequently, the revelation/memory of that moment where God intersected their lives, in a way they should never forget, dissipates. If an altar isn't built at such times, we yield that moment to a potential void of forgottenness.

Just as with words drawn in thin air by a skywriting plane, as time passes and the winds of adversity blow, the clarity of the message fades away. So we too easily lose *possession* of the promise and conviction wanes.

Imagine asking Abraham, "Has God promised you that you would possess this land?"

"Yes, He has."

"How do you know? Was it one day when suddenly you felt impressed that way?"

"No," he would say, "Come and I'll show you where it was." And he would lead you to a place and announce, "See that-- right there . . . that pile of stones? That's where I was. It happened about 25 years ago. God dealt with my heart, and I said, 'Okay, Lord. I receive Your promise.'" He could answer you as to how promise of God's purpose was nailed down in his own personal experience again and again.

You continue your interview: "Abraham, you seem to know the Lord pretty well. How'd it come about?" His answer begins as he leads the way to another site.

"See that place there?" He points across a valley, "There, between Bethel and Ai? That's where the Lord deepened my understanding of Him; where I began to know Him more intimately--by His name, if you will." He pauses, then continues: "I already knew that God was promising me *something*, but that altar is where I really came to know *Him*--the Living God, as He manifested Himself to me by *His name*."

"But Abraham, how come you've never gone home again--back to Haran, to your family there?"

"Simply because God told me, '*This* is my land!' "

"Don't you ever get homesick?"

"I have, just as anyone longs for things past. But God has called me *here*, and *here* I'll live. He told me this is where I was to stay--in His purpose."

"How did you make up your mind?"

Again, the patriarch answers: "God dealt with me. See, there's another pile of stones there. They testify to that fact! When that was 'nailed down,' as you say, it was done!"

"Abraham, even though you don't *have* it yet, you seem to really believe you're going to possess this land."

"Possess it? I've walked over the whole thing. God told me wherever my foot went, it was becoming mine! I believe that-- though it is mostly yet to be seen, I've 'seen' it with His eyes. It's coming!"

"So you have a good spiritual feeling about it?"

"No, feelings have little to do with it. But there *is* something to see--there's a pile of rocks right there. There's where I sealed and settled it with God--according to His Word and promise, which never fails!"

Listen to that conversation, Sir. And look at that line of altars. They've become milestones in the life of a man, marking his walk with God. And they become something else, too.

If a man wants to find out *where he's going*--how God's leading him--all he has to do to look into the future is to stop a minute, turn around, and see the trail of altars behind--the points of God's dealing with him until now. They indicate direction--because God isn't zig-zagging us through life in an arbitrary Keystone Cop chase. He's bringing each of us along a divinely-scheduled pathway . . . if we'll walk with Him. And if we'll "nail down" actual experiences by building altars, with time we can turn around at any point and check: "Is where I'm going in line with where He's been taking me?" And believe me, it always *will* be. Even though the Lord does do new things in our lives--"great and mighty things which we know not"--His dealings will always have roots in things He's done years ago; consistently in harmony with His past dealings and always in alignment with His Word.

This is the way to a solid sense of direction. It beats just flying along on whatever happens to be the current ear-tickling teaching or the latest point of social or religious excitement or some giddy exhilaration in your life. Altars built in your life become granite anchors. Abraham had them. And he became the prototype of how a man walks with God.

A Man's Altar of Priority

This altar of Abraham's was not a conventional arrangement of stones. But the purposed determination in Abraham's life in Genesis 14:16-18--as he is approached by two kings--focuses an altar-type encounter with God's representative.

The battle against the coalition of five hostile kings has been won by Abraham. His nephew, Lot, who had been kidnapped, has now been recovered. The story proceeds in the wake of this victory.

So he (Abraham) brought back all the goods, and also brought back his brother Lot and his goods, as well as the women and the people. And the King of Sodom went out to meet him at the Valley of Shaveh (that is, the King's Valley), after his return from the defeat of Chedorlaomer and the kings who were with him. Then Melchizedek King of Salem brought out bread and wine; he was the priest of God Most High. And he blessed him and said: "Blessed be Abram of God Most High, Possessor of heaven

47

*and earth; and blessed be God Most
High, who has delivered your enemies
into your hand." And he gave him a tithe
of all.*   *Genesis 14:16-20*

There's a strikingly interesting con-
trasting study in the two kings Abraham
meets, and strong instruction is in it for any
man.

First, the King of Sodom is a perfect
depiction of Satan--the king of hell. "Sodom" literally means "burnt or scorched."
This king was the leader of a hell-bent city,
destined to be destroyed by divine judg-
ment. Second, and in contrast, Melchizedek,
the King of Salem, ruled over the ancient
city of Salem (Jerusalem). This righteous
king is shown in the book of Hebrews as a
type of Jesus, a priest both preceding and
exceeding the Aaronic and Levitical priest-
hood. Melchizedek's name means "Prince
of Peace," a startling prophetic picture to
say the least. And now both kings come out
to meet Abraham.

You might say that, on one hand, Abraham is virtually approached by Satan
himself, and on the other, he is virtually
encountered by Jesus--the Priest of the
Most High God, our Great High Priest.

Abraham's confrontation by these two
kings teaches a great principle. Neither
you nor I will ever gain a spiritual victory
but that shortly thereafter we'll face a new

choice as to our priorities. There's something heady about spiritual triumph that begets an unusual vulnerability in the finest man, a vulnerability to distraction or deception. Remember, the surrounding text notes Abraham's warfare and rescue of Lot. Now this confrontation: This man's walk with God is going to face a real and practical decision. Where are his priorities when it comes to his devotion and his resources? It would be very easy for Abraham to make himself an independent prince who worships at his own shrine and only finances his own interests, but something else happens.

It's our wisdom to carefully tune to the message the Holy Spirit has for us in this episode. Our lesson is real: gain a spiritual victory, and you'll face a practical decision. Such situations have a way of *sealing* our priorities. They teach us that no degree of attainment bypasses the need for our faithfulness to the basics.

In Abraham's case--and in our study!-- worship and giving are shown to be inescapably important. Abraham doesn't play with them. He kept these priorities clear.

The subtlety of approach by the King of Sodom is almost demonic. He says, "Look, you can have all the plunder, just give us the people." That's Satan's way: "I'll give you anything, just let me control souls."

In contrast, Abraham had just secured

priorities with Melchizedek, who had come to him with bread and wine. Think of it! Our text is 2200 years before Christ, and precious principles still alive today are seen already speaking prophetically.

See Melchizedek, a picture of Christ Jesus Himself, bringing bread and wine to Abraham. Here's a perfect picture of our Lord calling us to worship, as we do when we commemorate the Lord's Supper and testify to His death on the Cross.

Abraham worships!

He faces down the King of Sodom with the words, "I've made my choice. I've lifted up my hand to the Most High God, Creator of heaven and earth." Then, Abraham rejects Sodom's king as he proposes making him rich on his terms. Next,

Abraham tithes!

Read it clearly; verse 20 says it all: "Abraham gave (Melchizedek) a tithe of all."

Brother, this is so powerfully significant in understanding a man's walk with God. Once we enter the pathway of discipleship, the only biblical response from an economic standpoint is the priority of our serving God with our money. The tithe is timeless as a testimony of this priority being fixed in a man's heart and life. *Everything is God's:* And my tithe indicates that all I have is His!!

When the King of Sodom says, "You can take everything, Abraham," Abraham's reply is, "I don't want anything that's got the smell of your life on it." The altar is in place. Heaven is exalted--hell is defeated!

TALK ABOUT IT! Chapter questions to discuss with a friend.

1) We are all grateful to the Lord for the many pastors, teachers, authors, and counselors who have helped shape our lives, but explain why it is those times *alone* with the Lord that make the biggest impact in changing our thinking and lifestyle. Share such an experience you've had alone with the Lord and its resulting benefits.

2) Society and modern-day media can make us think the word "destiny" refers to fairy tales or something that only happens to people who "live happily ever after." Yet, it is a wonderful truth that God has a destiny for each one of us to possess! Describe what the Lord has spoken to you about your own destiny.

CHAPTER FOUR:
THE PROCESS OF ALTARS–
THE CONSUMING OF FLESH

A Man's Altar of Perception

Have you ever faced dark times and wondered what God was doing with your life?

One of the most trying times of my earlier walk with God took place following one of the most glorious seasons of fruitfulness I'd ever known. Things had been "comin' up roses," as we say; but suddenly--in a matter of weeks--the forward movement and sense of blessing, which three years of labor had abounded, was now sunk in the doldrums of uncertainty and discouragement.

Officials holding office above me seemed doubtful about my efforts at serving. All momentum related to anything I was involved in was dragging to a halt. When I prayed, it seemed nothing happened. I didn't feel God had forsaken me, but I did have the feeling that I was either "washed up" or a "washout."

But during that season, I turned to the Word of God. I had no emotion whatsoever, but I would daily turn to the Scriptures and simply open God's Book to see if He might speak. And even though there were no explosive moments, as week followed week certain passages began to become impressed upon my heart as being "for me."

Slowly, I began to fix these things in my heart--like the stones set in place in the formation of an altar--and an entirely new perspective on my future began to come about.

I would later realize what was happening. God was creating a hiatus--an in-between-break--to differentiate between what had gone before and what He was getting ready to do. The whole season of seemingly slogging along--*but doing so as a measured walk with Him, however blind I was to His presence*--resulted in:

(1) Finding a new perspective on what He *was* doing and *intended* to do; and

(2) Discovering a pathway through the dark, and that He was always there even though I couldn't see Him.

This is very much what Abraham's experience teaches us. We're about to meet him as he comes to another altar encounter--one which brings perspective on God's long-term *purpose* for him, and God's constant *presence* with Him.

And he said, "Lord God, how shall I know that I will inherit it?" So He said to him, "Bring Me a three-year-old heifer, a three-year-old female goat, a three-year-old ram, a turtledove, and a young pigeon." Then he brought all these to Him and cut them in two, down the middle, and placed each piece opposite the other; but he did not cut the birds

in two.   And when the vultures came
down on the carcasses, Abraham drove
them away.   Now when the sun was
going down, a deep sleep fell upon
Abraham; and behold, horror and great
darkness fell upon him.   Then He said to
Abraham: "Know certainly that your
descendants will be strangers in a land
that is not theirs, and will serve them,
and they will afflict them four hundred
years.   And also the nation whom they
serve I will judge; afterward they shall
come out with great possessions.   Now
as for you, you shall go to your fathers
in peace; you shall be buried at a good
old age."   *Genesis 15:8-15*

Notice,   Abraham's   quest   for
perspective--for insight on God's timing
and assurance. "How shall I know that I
shall inherit the land?" He already had the
promise secured in hand, but he also had
a *problem*--a problem with seeing what he
thought God was going to do actually take
place as he expected.

See this, please, Abraham believes God;
he isn't saying, "Lord, I don't believe
You--Your promise is a dud!" But he's
saying, "Lord, in some way, I need to know
more what's happening. Please show me
how all this comes about." The Lord's
answer shouldn't surprise us. "Build an
altar, Abraham. Offer sacrifice."

Now it seems a corner is about to be

turned.

I won't be dogmatic about this, but even though altars had been built, not before this is there mention of Abraham offering a blood sacrifice. Because he had raised altars several times, I suppose most would preclude that he presented blood sacrifices there. But all the preceding times he raises an altar, each seems to be more of a monument to the Lord and a memorial to His dealing with Abraham. These towers of testimony had been places of worship, prayer, and fellowship. But now it seems Abraham is about to learn quite literally the role of "blood, sweat, and tears" when a man finds the fullest stages of divine purposes being worked out in his walk with God.

The revelation of God's blood covenant is manifest here. Abraham is about to gain deeper perspective; receiving a lesson in the fact that *God's ultimate means for possessing all promises* is through slain flesh and blood.

How does God fulfill these promises today?

To begin, He fulfills them all--every promise, every possibility--through Calvary; through the provisions inherent in the finished work of Christ on the Cross. The "slain flesh and blood" I just mentioned, which Abraham will only see as an early prophetic type, is an accomplished fact today. We are now recipients of provisions full and finally paid for through Jesus' death. The flesh slain is His, as the Son of God, and the blood shed is His as God's Lamb.

But let me say something, brother. As foundational as the work of Christ is, still--ultimately--any outworking of God's fullest purposes in you and me will at one point or another start cutting into our own flesh as well. That's what Jesus means when He calls us to "Take up your cross and follow Me" (Mark 10:21). This doesn't mean the Lord is leading us to a means of *earning* through suffering, agony, and misery, as though we would accomplish something by *works*. But rather, He calls us to *learn* (not earn) the power of His *grace* (not our works) to move through the darkness to discover new light!

The Lord is summoning all of us to discipleship: "Follow Me--to Calvary!" He'll be there to lead and teach us, but the only way to learn what Paul calls "the fellowship of His suffering" (Phil. 3:10) is to learn the kind of violent perseverance Abraham demonstrates here.

We need to grasp the dynamic lesson Genesis 15:11 unfolds.

After Abraham's sacrifice is made, wild birds begin to assail the carcasses sacrificed on the altar. Darkness is settling on the same. The sun has gone down and a deep sleep is shortly to fall on Abraham. There are two principles that distill here; things which are not uncommon when God is teaching men like you and me what it means to walk with Him on the pathway of the Cross.

First, just as the vultures attacked Abraham's sacrifice, in the same way our Adversary the devil will sweep in to attempt everything possible to prevent us from presenting our full sacrifice to God.

Second, like the darkening sun and the deep sleep, you'll experience some order of "blackout"--an inability to see what God is doing. The question rises: Where did God go?

You've had such blackout moments, haven't you? Times when you, like Abraham's "How shall I know," have said, "Lord, I want to know more about what You're doing--I don't understand." We affirm, "Lord, I believe You, so that's settled. Now can we move on with fulfilling the promise--soon?" But then it's as though the Lord replies, "You really want to learn? Okay, here we go."

Then, it's sacrifice.

Then discipleship deepens.

Then you find Him involving you in dealings which "cut flesh," removing carnality.

And hardly has this new discipling begun, when the next thing you know the Adversary is circling like a devouring vulture. He will do anything possible to block, stop, or swallow up our learning Christ's pathway of seeing the Cross applied to our lives in its promise-releasing power.

Certain New Testament parables use fowls to illustrate the workings of the powers of darkness; how Satan seeks to come and "eat up"--to remove what you or I have opened of ourselves and exposed to the Lord in sacrifice. But see Abraham beat those birds away, and remember his style when Satan tests your commitment.

Once you expose your full self to God, expect the Adversary to sweep down and say, "Heh, man, I've controlled this flesh of yours 'til now! This is my turf. I've got a right to snatch this away. God can have the 'spiritual' you, but I own the 'practical, daily duty, work and business' you! None of this 'everything under Jesus' Lordship' stuff! Besides, you're not worthy of this sacrifice anyway."

But when Satan comes, rise up, brother! Resist the devil, and he'll flee from you!! See Abraham drive the vultures back, protecting the sacrifice; and that, my dear friend, is our responsibility, too.

How tempting to say, "Well, I did my part. I made my sacrifice, and since then the devil's just been giving me a horrible time."

Listen, I *know* people are often plagued by the devil. But I would *love* to hear a lot more people say, "Yessir, the devil *has* been plaguing me, *but I've decided to plague him back!!* I'm gonna stand in spiritual warfare! I'm asking God to make those demons wish they had never touched me!"

I'm not minimizing our Adversary. But, my brother, I'm also persuaded that if we would rise up in the Name of Jesus;

• to stand straight, taking the Blood of the Cross,
• to move forward, singing--"in his face"--of the Blood of Jesus,

we would find Satan is not an unconquerable opponent. So, get on your feet! Begin to attack! And those "birds" will scatter.

Hallelujah!

Let's both rise and defend the sacrifice of discipleship which we've made!

Let God arise, let His enemies be scattered; let those also who hate Him flee before Him. As smoke is driven away, so drive them away; as wax melts before the fire, so let the wicked perish at the presence of God. But let the righteous be glad; let them rejoice before God; yes, let them rejoice exceedingly.
Psalm 68:1-3

Walking in the Dark

Then, the darkness came.

Sir, dark, black times come for us all. There are times in a man's walk with God that you can't see God at all! You feel like the Lord has gone to the far side of the Universe, leaving you sitting in a personal crisis of some kind. But my brother, when you face those times, as I have too, you'll do well to remember the wisdom of Psalm 18.

And He (the Lord) rode upon a cherub, and flew; He flew upon the wings of the wind. He made darkness His secret place; His canopy around Him was dark waters and thick clouds of the skies.
Psalm 18:10-11

Listen to it! God *dwells* in the darkness! We serve a God who works in the dark. He did so at Creation. He did it at Israel's deliverance from Egypt. He did so at the Cross. And just as at those times, so He still will work creatively, redemptively, and victoriously in our dark times. Remember,

• When we can't see *anything,* He sees *everything.*

• When we are most vulnerable, He is most powerful.

• The darkness that makes you feel He's at the *greatest distance* is the time when He is the *most near.*

This psalm says that God puts on darkness as a coat; stepping inside your darkness, He will wear it like a garment. *He is in there with you!!*

A horror of great darkness came on Abraham, but it was then and there that the Lord began to speak to him. It's in the middle of his darkness that God is, in effect, saying: "Now, I'm going to explain my timing, Abraham. I'm going to keep My promise to you, but it's not going to be on your schedule or work out the way you thought."

Have you ever had God say something like that to you? Sure you have. And it shouldn't ever disappoint us, because God isn't being contrary or capricious, or opposing our ways just to prove He's the Boss. But He is working in ways transcending ours; embracing purposes far more expansive than our life and circumstance alone.

This text introduces us to a grand concept. Abraham is beginning to see the reason God is taking longer in his program of fulfillment, and it's because what He's doing in Abraham involves God's purposes with many other peoples.

Can you capture this truth? God is using us *amid* His purposes, not *apart* from them!

This is extremely profound. And profoundly important.

God's dealings with Abraham were not just for Abraham's sake, though he was certainly large on God's agenda and much on God's heart. But God's dealings with Abraham were not just for him and his family, or even for the nation of Israel--as central as that nation was and is to God's purposes. The Lord enlarges Abraham's perspective, showing him how he fits in with things God is doing which encompass nations and span centuries.

Think of it! See how God's dealings with this one man take into account the future of God's seeking to bring entire *nations* to repentance! The phrase from Genesis 15:16, "The iniquity of the Amorites is not yet complete," not only reflects God's longsuffering with an entire nation--His gift of opportunity for their repentance; but this reveals His synchronous, multi-layered dealings with all humanity through a cause-and-effect circuit that could blow our human minds' capacity to comprehend!

Sir, we're instruments in the hands of a redeeming God who wants to use us--each one--to impact far more than we could ever dream! Just as God says, "Abraham, My dealing with you incorporates the flow of My dealings with nations and peoples yet to come," so, my brother, none of us lives or dies to himself.

Most of us have seen the delightful old film, *It's a Wonderful Life*; a kind, humanistic parable involving a man who in the midst of being driven to the brink of suicide is intercepted by an angel. The theology of the dramatization isn't quite biblical, but the central concept of the movie certainly is: the lives of multitudes would have been tragically different if he had never been born. So it is, a man's walk with God is not for his own sake alone, but to impact entire communities, peoples, nations. That's why we need to trust the Lord's timing when promised fulfillment sometimes seems slow. It's often simply because of larger issues than your or my personal circumstance alone--issues involving great interweavings of things He's doing in your life as it eventually intersects other lives.

So, don't let yourself be pinched into a pigeon-hole-box way of thinking about the Lord's working in you, toward you, or through you. As God said to Abraham, "I will make your name *great*." Remember--He wants you and me to hear Him, because He's saying the same thing to us: "I have great purposes for you."

This is absolutely biblical! Make no mistake, God is up to great things in our lives! Listen to the Apostle Paul's prayerful appeal: *"The eyes of your understanding being enlightened; that you may know ... the exceeding greatness of His power toward us"* (Eph. 1:18-19).

Further, the same passage says that it's going to take "the ages to come" for God to bring us to fully see "the exceeding riches of His grace" (Eph. 2:7). Yes, Sir, God *is* up to something with men who choose to walk with Him. He has big things He's doing with us.

God: "Abraham, look, it's like the stars . . . You can't count them all, but what

I'm doing is BIG" (Gen. 15:5).

Abraham: "But God, when, how?" (Gen. 15:8).

God: "This is the way, Abraham. It's a pathway to the stars, but it moves through the blood of sacrifice, the battle against the birds, and via a way of darkness--a way of learning time elements that you don't understand.

"But when it's all over," the Lord teaches Abraham, "I'm going to fulfill the huge dimensions of purpose I've promised and measured to you. I am your shield, your exceedingly great reward--your Defender and your Fulfiller."

Listen to those words as they address us.

And let's be consumed by God's way of thinking, learning through the darkness to see His perspective. It's *all* and *always* working together for good for men who choose to walk with Him!

TALK ABOUT IT! Chapter questions to discuss with a friend.

1) Have you ever gone through a "dark time" of discouragement or personal crisis when you felt like God was nowhere in sight--a time when, despite your efforts to follow God's way, the Adversary seemed to swarm around you like flies? Share something the "Lord Who Works in the Dark" taught you through one of these darkness experiences.

2) Like the vultures which sought to attack Abraham's sacrifice, Satan will test the commitment you've just made to spend more time in His presence. Let's be prepared for his attack and have our battle weapons ready! (James 4:7; Eph. 6:10-18). Share some of your victories in scattering the devil's "vultures" in your life.

CHAPTER FIVE:
A MAN'S WALK . . .
UNTO SETTLED TRUST

A clearly marked trail of six altars in Abraham's life is now in place, and the *process of progress* cannot help but encourage you and me as men seeking a walk with God. We are tracing the way to liveable, practical, faith-filled, and dynamic life in Christ--and we haven't hit a "religious" snag yet. Contrary to the suppositions of many unbelievers, as well as contrary to the legalistic formulas of many Christians, spirituality is neither "otherworldly," nor is it a rigid, mechanical lifestyle. As we follow Abraham's footsteps, exactly as we're taught to view his human modeling of warm-blooded holiness (Rom. 4:12), all the pieces begin to fit together.

• An ordinary man can become God's "extraordinary";

• A fearful man can find God's dynamic;

• A stumbling man can find sure footing;

• A growing man can learn God's priorities;

• A questioning man can learn holy certainty; and now we'll see--

• An imperfect man can be formed through God's perfecting!

A Man's Altar of Perfecting

Now, there are two altars which bring us to the conclusion of our study of Abraham's pathway of progress in God's grace, and I'm calling them "A Man's Altars of Perfecting." Foremost in our approach to these incidents, with which God puts completing touches on Abraham's understanding of his covenant with Him, is that we not be intimidated by the word "perfecting."

Various translations of the Bible have intermittently used this word, not to describe accomplished perfection but to describe the advancing path of maturity--the "I'm-gonna-keep-on-growing-in-Christ-for-a-lifetime" pathway. The settling factors which establish a man's walk on such a path are finally rooted in two giant truths. These are "cutting edge" truths--both which literally bring us "under the knife of divine surgery." And even though the usual figure of exploratory or major "surgery" has a way of striking us as negative, *corrective surgery* shouldn't.

Think of the difference.

In one procedure--the kind we fear--the body is cut, organs or limbs removed, and then--as tragically is often the case--the patient still doesn't survive. But *corrective* surgery results in new *capacities* being realized, originally intended *efficiency* released, and new *dimensions* for joyous living opened up.

This is the concept of "perfecting" as we examine Abraham's learning of lessons for our own growth in God's way. These altars bring us to understanding that the essence of His program of "perfection" is *not* so much in accomplishment, attainment, or verified excellence, as it is in our settled, certain *direction*--at all times.

Remember that, my brother. Let these words be fixed in your soul for your lifetime in Christ: *God is not so interested in my perfection as He is in my direction!* What happened with Abraham at these last two altar encounters became the capstone on his earlier life of learning God's way, and secured his movement in God's will for the rest of his earthly walk.

"Perfecting": Step One

It's an interesting fact that, chronologically, these two altar encounters (which are separated by only a few years) are early enough in Abraham's life that more than a full one-third of his years follow without any question or bewilderment. In short: There *is* a place in Christ where life-patterns become fixed, faith becomes settled, but the adventure of ongoing advancement in God never becomes boring, disinteresting, or dull. So it *is* possible, brother. You and I *can* learn a walk with God that becomes "perfected" unto solidity--and joy!

Let's read together the first of these last two "perfecting" encounters:

> When Abram was ninety-nine years old, the Lord appeared to Abram and said to him, "I am Almighty God; walk before Me and be blameless. And I will make My covenant between Me and you, and will multiply you exceedingly."

> Then Abram fell on his face, and God talked with him, saying: "As for Me, behold, My covenant is with you, and you shall be a father of many nations. No longer shall your name be called Abram, but your name shall be Abraham; for I have made you a father of many nations. I will make you exceedingly fruitful; and I will make nations of you, and kings shall come from you. And I will establish My covenant between Me and you and your descendants after you in their generations, for an everlasting covenant, to be God to you and your descendants after you. Also I give to you and your descendants after you the land in which you are a stranger, all the land of Canaan, as an everlasting possession; and I will be their God."

> And God said to Abraham: "As for you, you shall keep My covenant, you and your descendants after you throughout their generations. This is My covenant which you shall keep, between Me and

you and your descendants after you:
Every male child among you shall be
circumcised; and you shall be circum-
cised in the flesh of your foreskins, and
it shall be a sign of the covenant be-
tween Me and you." Genesis 17:1-11

I want to literally "cut" to the core of the message this "altar" of Abraham's contains. The profundity of the implications involved in the ancient rite of circumcision is too grand to elaborate here. In fact, one of our future books in this series for men will be given in entirety to discussing the power-principles hidden in the Old Testament covenant practice of circumcision, which was religiously observed until New Testament times. But at the heart of this practice is God's call that we surrender to the cutting away of our flesh; that we submit to the sword of His Word which calls us away from carnal indulgence and fleshly mindedness, and permits the Holy Spirit to *excise the unnecessary.*

Just as the removing of the fleshly foreskin of the body in no way inhibits future reproductivity, God only calls for us to submit to the removal of habits, ways of thought, modes of behavior, and bent attitudes--any one of which (and certainly *all* together)--will reduce our fruitfulness, block our progress or hinder our potential for effectiveness in our lives and living.

Of course we always have a choice. You can back off and say, "I don't want to have any of that 'cutting' in my heart!" But remember, if we do, we'll have to live with the consequences of bypassing that "altar" call. We'll find in time the undesirability of the excess baggage, the bondage, and the burdens of flesh. Instead, let the circumcision of your heart reveal the power of the Holy Spirit, who brings instead His fruit, His love, His joy, His peace, and so much more. So Abraham's "altar" of circumcision is the picture of the power of God's Word through the Holy Spirit's ministry to carve away the unnecessary, the carnal, the unproductive.

And with that seventh altar, we come to the eighth and last altar we'll study in Abraham's life. It's the second of two "altars of perfecting," but this one became at one and the same time the greatest test and the greatest victory of Abraham's faith.

Now it came to pass after these things that God tested Abraham, and said to him, "Abraham!" And he said, "Here I am." Then He said, "Take now your son, your only son Isaac, whom you love, and go to the land of Moriah, and offer him there as a burnt offering on one of the mountains of which I shall tell you." So Abraham rose early in the morning and saddled his donkey, and took two of his young men with him, and Isaac his son; and he split the wood for the burnt offering, and arose and went to the place of which God had told him.

Then on the third day Abraham lifted his eyes and saw the place afar off.

And Abraham said to his young men, "Stay here with the donkey; the lad and I will go yonder and worship, and we will come back to you."

So Abraham took the wood of the burnt offering and laid it on Isaac his son; and he took the fire in his hand, and a knife, and the two of them went together.

But Isaac spoke to Abraham his father and said, "My father!" And he said, "Here I am, my son." Then he said, "Look, the fire and the wood, but where is the lamb for a burnt offering?"

And Abraham said, "My son, God will provide for Himself the lamb for a burnt offering." So the two of them went together.

Then they came to the place of which God had told him. And Abraham built an altar there and placed the wood in order; and he bound Isaac his son and laid him on the altar, upon the wood.

And Abraham stretched out his hand and took the knife to slay his son.

But the Angel of the Lord called to him from heaven and said, "Abraham, Abraham!" So he said, "Here I am."

And He said, "Do not lay your hand on the lad, or do anything to him; for now I know that you fear God, since you have not withheld your son, your only son, from Me.''

Then Abraham lifted his eyes and looked, and there behind him was a ram caught in a thicket by its horns. So Abraham went and took the ram, and offered it up for a burnt offering instead of his son.
Genesis 22:1-13

There is possibly no more tender story in all the Bible short of the ultimate story this even prophesies: the sacrifice by Almighty God of His own, His only Son on the Cross. Abraham was not only experiencing the soul-jarring summons to sacrifice, he was struggling with a concept which went at cross purposes to everything He knew of God. You see, Abraham's God didn't demand human sacrifice as the surrounding pagan world practiced it. But God is leading Abraham, not merely to the top of Mount Moriah, He is bringing him to the pinnacle of understanding. It's the place God wants to bring every man eventually--every man who wants to walk with God.

GOD WANTS TO BRING YOU AND ME TO:

1. THE PLACE WHERE WE ARE WILLING TO TRUST *HIM*, EVEN WHEN EVERYTHING AROUND SEEMS TO SUGGEST HE HAS CHANGED HIS WAYS; AND TO

2. THE PLACE WHERE THERE IS NOTHING SO TREASURED BY US THAT WE ARE UNWILLING TO SURRENDER IT COMPLETELY TO HIS HANDS--EVEN TO EXTINCTION.

There are a thousand lessons in this incredibly wonderful passage of Scripture. Abraham's faith rose to action, believing that even if he *did* slay Isaac in obedience to God, the Almighty Faithful One would mightily, gloriously--and in line with His full promises for the future--raise Isaac from the dead!! (See Hebrews 11:18-19, which says exactly that!)

This is the ultimate *perfecting* in a man's walk with God--his arrival at a place of total trust, complete assurance: God will never fail His promises! God will never change His nature!

But the arrival at this peak in growth is not readily attained. It's the fruitage born from a growing, developing, progressing process of faith's lessons--at altars. For it is in the building of altars, in the encountering of God at distinct times in distinct ways, that a man's walk with God comes to increase and fruition.

And altar-building is never easy.

We're drawing to a conclusion, and I want to leave you with a vision of yourself as a lifelong builder of altars. I'm still building, and so is every man I know who has chosen to walk with God. But as you chart that course--like Abraham who walked this pathway of faith before us--I want to urge the remembrance of this practical counsel: There are basic keys to living as an altar-builder.

How do you build an altar? A number of things come to mind, but the thing that most impresses me about altars, as symbolized in the stone mounds arranged by the patriarchs like Abraham, is that *altars are built from hard things*.

Rocks.

The tough.

The unyielding situation.

A single difficulty, or a complete collection of hard things in life, can set up the possibility of an altar being formed.

This analogy of rocks being like life's "hard things" relates to the fact that rocks are the natural result of certain physical processes which formed them. I'm not an expert in geology, but I've read enough to know that stones or splinters of rock--granite and various other minerals--are the result of two primary forces:

(1) volcanic action or explosions, which

melt, cool, shape, and hurl rocks; and

(2) extreme temperatures, hot and cold, which crack and shatter larger masses of rock to smaller rocks.

For each of us, the building of an altar is often basically our choice to collect "hard things"--tough things that are a result of either explosions or extremities in our lives--and to bring them into arrangement before God.

Sometimes, things "blow up in our faces"--hard things that we need to learn how to take to the Lord. Other times freezing cold (loneliness, rejection, depression) or emotional exception (anger, bitterness, harsh words) fill our lives with hard things. But this "altar lesson" calls us to learn what to do with those tough things. Our response will determine whether an altar will be erected, and the face of God sought, or if we'll try to handle the "roles" in other ways.

For one thing, we can just carry them--try to handle them as burdens of our own. Unsurrendered to "altar-building," they're an unwieldy burden, but many people have whole collections of hard things! "Hey, I've got problems you've never even seen before! In fact, I've polished up some of mine for display! Wanna see 'em?" Unarranged in prayer before God, our "hard things" can be paraded for their special designs and rare qualities, but they'll never be changed . . .

only collected.

Another thing one can do with life's "hard things" is to throw them at other people. Like a rock, a past pain or present difficulty can be hurled in anger: "If I've got a problem, it's gonna be yours, too!" And, Bammm!!

Or, life's hard things can simply be left lying there . . . neglected, as though to pretend they will go away on their own. But if not arranged before God in altar-building, hard things lying on the ground--undealt with--will soon cut someone's feet or trip another passerby. Passivity toward hard things doesn't work. Like rocks on a roadway, they'll remain a scattered mess in the path or split a tire of an unsuspecting driver.

God didn't intend any of us to be damaged by life's rocky hard things. They're simply a part of the world that we're living in. But it *is* God's intent to convert life's tough things to blessings; to fulfill His Word that "all things *do* work together for good for those who love God and are called according to His purpose." For this to happen, we need to take such "rocks" and turn them into altars--placing them before Him and arranging them in order.

And when you do, one thing remains.

As with ancient times, where the sacrifice was poured out on the altar, there's a contemporary counterpart for our action.

After the altar is built, we need: *to pour out our hearts!*

• Whatever the difficulty, open your heart completely.

• Whatever the frustration, declare your feelings without hesitation.

• Whatever the pain, let its fullness be laid in His presence.

• Whatever the anger, disappointment, or struggle--let your whole life be placed in His hands as you pour your heart's cry before Him.

And as you do, you'll find our Father's ability to deal with a heart that's opened itself--that's bared its fullest cry to Him.

So, the secret is to see life's hard things for what they are. They're the product of explosions and extremities--not to be carried, collected or thrown, but to be arranged before the Father. Then, to allow our heart to be poured out over the matter--

for His healing our hurt,

for His teaching our mind,

for His correcting our perspective,

for His soothing our soul,

for His removing our fears,

for His leading us beyond our rockiness into His revelation.

And as He reveals Himself, we'll find but another blessing that results when a person decides to walk with God. We'll find the power of altars to alter! To change our heart, charge us with wisdom, and call us with faith into His future for us.

That's why we all have this unalterable need of an altar.

It's the timeless pathway of all who would learn to walk with the Almighty--changed by His power to learn of His changeless grace and abounding purpose for us.

For you.

TALK ABOUT IT! Chapter questions to discuss with a friend.

1) Find a partner and pray together over the current "hard things"--burdens in your life--that need to be laid at Jesus' feet; name people before the Father in prayer and declare your forgiveness of them; ask the Lord to reveal ways for you to begin reconciliation with those with whom fellowship has been broken.

2) We have learned in our study that a better rendering of the biblical word "perfection" is "maturity." God wants us to continue to "grow up" in His way. List some life-patterns or areas you wish to grow in--mature in--during this season of your life.

DEVOTIONS

In CHAPTERS 12 through 22 of

GENESIS

Contributed by Bob Anderson

This devotional covers a critical section of Scripture. In Chapters 12 - 22 of the book of Genesis the Christian faith finds its deepest moorings: in the life of Abraham, the man referred to by the Apostle Paul as "the father of all those who believe"–those of us who walk by faith (cf. Romans 4:11).

Since Genesis is the "Book of Beginnings," our prayer is that this devotional in the life of Abraham will earmark the beginning of a whole new dimension in your walk with God.

(It is suggested that this devotional be used for stimulating discussion and prayer within a small group of men meeting regularly.)

☐ **Today's Text: Genesis 12:1- 3** *(key v. 1)*

1 **Today's Truth:** Abraham could have cleaved to physical "security and predictability" by remaining in his father's house and thus retaining control of his life. But laying all this down from a pure motive of obedience to God, he inherited wealth and eternal glory far beyond what his mind could envision.

Today's Thoughts: _____

_____

_____

☐ **Today's Text: Genesis 12:4-9** *(key v.4)*

2 **Today's Truth:** We can sometimes feel as though the season in life wherein God can use us has passed. But Abraham was already 75 years old when he began God's faith-walk adventure!

Today's Thoughts: _____

_____

_____

☐ **Today's Text: Genesis 12:10-20** *(key v. 17)*

3 **Today's Truth:** Abraham's sin of lying to Pharaoh's house adversely affected other lives. For this man, who would become *a blessing to nations*, this was a crucial lesson–one he would need to learn again–that of seeing how his moral decisions impacted others.

Today's Thoughts: _____

_____

_____

☐ **Today's Text: Genesis 13:1-4** *(key v. 4)*

4 **Today's Truth:** Abraham returned back to the beginning point of his journey but with new insight. His unhappy encounter with Pharaoh must have left him with a fresh reminder that doing things his own way instead of God's way will certainly lead to disaster.

Today's Thoughts: ―――――――――――
――――――――――――――――――――――
――――――――――――――――――――――

☐ **Today's Text: Genesis 13:5-13** *(key vv. 8-9)*

5 **Today's Truth:** Abraham avoids his former pattern of seizing control to protect his own interests. This time he releases control and prefers his nephew over his own desires.

Today's Thoughts: ―――――――――――
――――――――――――――――――――――
――――――――――――――――――――――

☐ **Today's Text: Genesis 13:14-18** *(key v. 14)*

6 **Today's Truth:** Abraham trusted God to take care of him and didn't seize the better grazing land from Lot–even though his culture would grant him such a right as the elder family member. Now God reminded him of the larger picture: we're not talking about grazing land, we're talking *destiny!*

Today's Thoughts:―――――――――――
――――――――――――――――――――――
――――――――――――――――――――――

☐ **Today's Text: Genesis 14:1-16** *(key v. 14)*

7 **Today's Truth:** This is a new side to Abraham we've never seen before: a man of military skill and courage. His experience in following God by faith ignited new strength and confidence which may have been a surprise even to him as it emerged.

Today's Thoughts: _____

_____

_____

☐ **Today's Text: Genesis 14:17-24** *(key v. 22)*

8 **Today's Truth:** As soon as Abraham returned from a victorious battle, it would seem Heaven and Hell both approached him seeking his allegiance. With danger now abated, it could be easy to compromise with the spirit of this world. But Abraham's commitment to God was firm.

Today's Thoughts: _____

_____

_____

☐ **Today's Text: Genesis 15:1-6** *(key v. 6)*

9 **Today's Truth:** Abraham wanted a logical explanation for his future—"Will Eliezer be my heir, God?"—that old control hang-up again. But as God reaffirmed His miracle method, Abraham believed. This lesson of releasing control to God had to be learned once again at a deeper dimension.

Today's Thoughts: _____

_____

_____

☐ **Today's Text: Genesis 15:7-16** *(key vv. 12-13)*

10 **Today's Truth:** Sometimes we receive the greatest revelations, wisdom, and comfort from the Lord during times of great horror and darkness. We may not understand all that God is doing in our lives at the present, but God encompasses all of time and sees well beyond our finite perspective.

Today's Thoughts: _____

_____

_____

☐ **Today's Text: Genesis 15:17-21** *(key v. 17)*

11 **Today's Truth:** When flesh is offered up in sacrifice to God, the Lord's revival fire will then burn in the midst of our lives. This typified Abraham's life: his fleshly ways were sacrificed so that God's redemptive plan could unfold through him.

Today's Thoughts: _____

_____

_____

☐ **Today's Text: Genesis 16:1-5** *(key v. 2)*

12 **Today's Truth:** Abraham was tempted to help God fulfill His promise. Maybe God, who tarried ''too long'' in bringing forth His promise, might be blessed by a helping hand! Hagar must be the answer! But again, the best human efforts to do God's work fall woefully short of His glory.

Today's Thoughts: _____

_____

_____

☐ **Today's Text: Genesis 16:6-10** *(key v. 10)*

13 **Today's Truth:** The Lord's tender lovingkindness was even shown to Hagar, who was unrelated to God's redemptive plan. Even though she was not to be the mother of the promised heir, still, God's words of comfort directed her to believe for *her own* destiny.

Today's Thoughts: _____

_____

_____

☐ **Today's Text: Genesis 16:11-16** *(key v. 13)*

14 **Today's Truth:** Although Hagar was an Egyptian, she called upon her master's God. Despite the present conflict, something of the glory of the Lord must have shown through Abraham's and Sarah's lives for her to forsake her ancestors' gods and trust in the God of Abraham.

Today's Thoughts: _____

_____

_____

☐ **Today's Text: Genesis 17:1-8** *(key v. 5)*

15 **Today's Truth:** God changed Abram's name ("Exalted Father") to Abraham ("Father of a Multitude"). It was the added breath mark, the Hebrew syllable "ha," that made all the difference in the world–because it was God's Breath on him begetting new character and destiny.

Today's Thoughts: _____

_____

_____

☐ **Today's Text: Genesis 17:9-14** *(key v. 10)*

16 **Today's Truth:** The rite of circumcision zeroed in on two critical issues: (1) God's people were to cut away their fleshly dependence; and (2) the fulfillment of God's promise would come through human flesh–but flesh deeply touched, even cut into, by God's intervention.

Today's Thoughts: _____

_____

_____

☐ **Today's Text: Genesis 17:15-27** *(key v. 17)*

17 **Today's Truth:** Abraham laughed not because of unbelief but because of how amazing the promise seemed to him. Yet even though he laughed, and pleaded again that Ishmael might be the son of promise (v. 18), God still called Abraham "a man of faith."

Today's Thoughts: _____

_____

_____

☐ **Today's Text: Genesis 18:1-15** *(key v. 12)*

18 **Today's Truth:** It's interesting to note the Lord's harsher reaction to Sarah's laughter compared to when Abraham laughed. It is evident that Sarah was still set in unbelief, not merely amazement.

Today's Thoughts:_____

_____

_____

☐ **Today's Text: Genesis 18:16-33** *(key v. 32)*

19 **Today's Truth:** Abraham interceded for the preservation of Sodom. But in this unique negotiating process, it was Abraham, not the Lord, who ended the negotiations.

Today's Thoughts: _____

_____

_____

☐ **Today's Text: Genesis 19:1-29** *(key v. 16)*

20 **Today's Truth:** Apparently, other than Lot and his family, no other righteous persons were found in Sodom. Could it be that other righteous people *had* lived in Sodom but had left in disgust instead of remaining to impact the wicked city for righteousness and thereby alter its future?

Today's Thoughts: _____

_____

_____

☐ **Today's Text: Genesis 19:30-38** *(key v. 31)*

21 **Today's Truth:** The girls incorrectly assumed that God could not provide husbands for them since their homeland had been destroyed. So they "took control" of the situation and their incestuous relationships produced two sons whose descendents became the enemies of the descendents of Abraham. The Moabites and Ammonites would become two of the greatest snares to the Nation of Israel.

Today's Thoughts: _____

_____

_____

☐ **Today's Text: Genesis 20:1-7** *(key v. 2)*

22 **Today's Truth:** One of the challenges of faith is to "connect all the dots"–meaning if we believe God can do a miracle in one area of life, we sometimes fail to believe He can be as proficient in another. Abraham believed God could provide Isaac as promised, but he failed to believe God would protect him in the midst of danger.

Today's Thoughts: _____

_____

_____

☐ **Today's Text: Genesis 20:8-18** *(key v. 17)*

23 **Today's Truth:** As imperfect as Abraham was, he was, nonetheless, a man of faith who interceded for others. His being a blessing was both at a personal level as well as at an international level.

Today's Thoughts: _____

_____

_____

☐ **Today's Text: Genesis 21:1-7** *(key v. 3)*

24 **Today's Truth:** Isaac means "laughter." Abraham and Sarah had laughed in struggling to imagine the impossible. Now the laughter is born from joy.

Today's Thoughts: _____

_____

_____

☐ **Today's Text: Genesis 21:8-14** *(key v. 12)*

25 **Today's Truth:** God Almighty told Abraham, the Father of Israel, to listen to his wife and comply with what she said. Yes, there were unique circumstances in this case, but spiritual headship embraces attentive listening to the words, heart, and vision of one's wife. Always.

Today's Thoughts: ─────────────

_____

_____

☐ **Today's Text: Genesis 21:15-21** *(key v. 17)*

26 **Today's Truth:** It's touching that God "heard the voice of the lad." No voice is without significance. God takes seriously anyone who calls upon Him, no matter how weak or small that voice may be.

Today's Thoughts: ─────────────

_____

_____

☐ **Today's Text: Genesis 21:22-34** *(key v. 33)*

27 **Today's Truth:** Our study in the book described an altar as being potentially anything. Here Abraham plants a tamarisk tree and calls on the Name of the Lord.

Today's Thoughts: ─────────────

_____

_____

☐ **Today's Text: Genesis 22:1-8** *(key v. 8)*

28 **Today's Truth:** Abraham's mind must have been reeling! "My son–a human sacrifice!" Yet by now, Abraham's seasoned faith had learned that God's plans transcend human limitations and what our eyes alone can see.

Today's Thoughts: ⎯⎯⎯⎯⎯⎯⎯⎯
⎯⎯⎯⎯⎯⎯⎯⎯⎯⎯⎯⎯⎯⎯⎯⎯⎯⎯
⎯⎯⎯⎯⎯⎯⎯⎯⎯⎯⎯⎯⎯⎯⎯⎯⎯⎯

☐ **Today's Text: Genesis 22:9-14** *(key v. 14)*

29 **Today's Truth:** The dramatic rescue of Isaac now passed, Abraham calls the place "The-Lord-Will-Provide." But was this man of faith amazed? He himself had predicted in verse 8 that "God will provide." One can imagine Abraham breathing a sigh of relief, "Well, it was a close one, but He came through, *again* . . . as He *always* does!"

Today's Thoughts: ⎯⎯⎯⎯⎯⎯⎯⎯
⎯⎯⎯⎯⎯⎯⎯⎯⎯⎯⎯⎯⎯⎯⎯⎯⎯⎯
⎯⎯⎯⎯⎯⎯⎯⎯⎯⎯⎯⎯⎯⎯⎯⎯⎯⎯

☐ **Today's Text: Genesis 22:15-17** *(key v. 17)*

30 **Today's Truth:** Abraham began by trying to control events in his life. Now in the biggest test of all, he had totally relinquished control to God. And the reward was astronomical.

Today's Thoughts: ⎯⎯⎯⎯⎯⎯⎯⎯
⎯⎯⎯⎯⎯⎯⎯⎯⎯⎯⎯⎯⎯⎯⎯⎯⎯⎯
⎯⎯⎯⎯⎯⎯⎯⎯⎯⎯⎯⎯⎯⎯⎯⎯⎯⎯

☐ **Today's Text: Genesis 22:18-24** *(key v. 18)*

31 **Today's Truth:** God says literally that the entire planet will be profoundly blessed through Abraham's descendants because of his obedience to God. What an incredible bargain! For obedience that took only minutes to fulfill, centuries of blessing would cover the earth!

Today's Thoughts: _____

_____

_____

Please note:

Our devotional covers Chapters 12 through 22 of the book of Genesis because it is within these chapters that Abraham's life-long pursuit of God's will is recorded, while Chapters 23 - 25 record the final key events in Abraham's life. Chapter 23 tells us of details surrounding Sarah's death and burial; Chapter 24 tells the story of Abraham's role in securing a bride for Isaac; and Chapter 25 is the account of Abraham's death.

For a comparative study, the following additional verses of New Testament Scripture may be referred to: John 8:39-58; Romans 4:1-25; Galatians 3:1-18; Hebrews 7:1-9; and Hebrews 11:8-19.

Additional Resources for Biblical Manhood. . .

BOOKS

A MAN'S STARTING PLACE

This first book in the "Power-to-Become" Book-Pak series is a study of how men become mature in Christ through relationships with God, their spouse, and with other men. It is available individually or with its companion audio tape.* **Book only: AMSP $3.95**
Book & Tape: BP01 $7.95

A MAN'S CONFIDENCE

This second book in the "Power-to-Become" Book-Pak series is a study of how men become confident in life through mastering guilt.*

Book only: AMC $3.95
Book & Tape: BP02 $7.95

For subscription orders or quantity discounts for the "Power-to-Become" Books or Book-Pak series for use in personal or group studies, call (818) 779-8180 or (800) 776-8180.

NEWBORN

This book outlines the basic elements in a growing life with Jesus and discusses the believer's relationship to God, how the Bible can help in one's spiritual journey, types of baptism, and the need for spending time with other believers. **NBN $ 3.95**

DAYBREAK: Walking With Christ Every Day

Transforms generalized exhortations about "daily devotions" into a workable, non-legalistic set of specifics as to how the earnest believer can develop a fulfilling devotional prayer life. **DBK $ 2.95**

PRAYERPATH

Pastor Hayford takes the reader step by step along the pathway of prayer, examining the things Jesus taught about how to live and grow in vital faith, as well as how to pray for spiritual breakthrough at a global dimension. **PRP $ 3.95**

SPIRIT-FILLED:
The Overflowing Power of the Holy Spirit

Practical instruction on the Person and Power of the Spirit, teaching the enablement and resources of spiritual gifts and graces. Encourages the reader to open to the fullness of the Spirit of Christ, and shows how to maintain wisdom and balance in daily Spirit-filled living. **SFL $ 3.95**

TAKING HOLD OF TOMORROW

The practical principles of "Possessing the

Promised Land," found in the story of Joshua, encourage the reader to move forward and actively take hold of God's promises in life. This Angel Award winning book teaches the believer about spiritual warfare, submission, personal holiness, and obedience. *(Regularly $12.95)*
THT $ 9.95

This same subject is presented in an 8-tape audio album and in a series of 4 videotapes.
Audio SC130 $34   Video PYTVS $65

REBUILDING THE REAL YOU

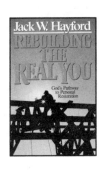

Just as Nehemiah went to Jerusalem with all the provisions he would need to rebuild the walls of the city, so the Holy Spirit comes with all that is needed to restore a broken personality. *(Regularly $8.95)*
RRY02 $7.95

The same subject is presented in 11 audio tapes or 6 videotapes.   **Audio SC046 $49.00**
Video RTWVS $99.00

AUDIO CASSETTE MINI-ALBUMS (2 tapes)

Honest to God	**SC122**	**$8**
Redeeming Relationships for Men & Women	**SC177**	**$8**
Why Sex Sins Are Worse Than Others	**SC179**	**$8**
How God Uses Men	**SC223**	**$8**

A Father's Approval	**SC225**	**$8**
Resisting the Devil	**SC231**	**$8**
The War in Your Life and World	**SC367**	**$8**
How to Recession-Proof Your Home	**SC369**	**$8**
Safe Sex!	**SC448**	**$8**
The Leader Jesus Trusts	**SC461**	**$8**

AUDIO CASSETTE ALBUMS (# of tapes)

Cleansed for the Master's Use (3)	**SC377**	**$13**
Becoming God's Man (4)	**SC457**	**$17**
Fixing Family Fractures (4)	**SC217**	**$17**
The Power of Blessing (4)	**SC395**	**$17**
Men's Seminars 1990-91 (10)	**MSEM**	**$42**
Premarital Series (12)	**PM02**	**$50**
A Family Encyclopedia (24)	**SC233**	**$99**

VHS VIDEO ALBUMS

Why Sex Sins Are Worse Than Others	**WSSV**	**$19**
Divorce and the People of God	**DIVV**	**$19**
Earthly Search for a Heavenly Father	**ESFV**	**$19**

Add 15% for shipping and handling.
California residents add 8.25% sales tax.

*Request your **free** Resource Catalog.*

**Call Living Way Ministries Resources
at (818) 779-8180 or (800) 776-8180.**